Maths
made easy

Key Stage 2
Ages 9–10
Advanced

Author John Kennedy
Consultant Sean McArdle

Certificate

Congratulations to ....
(write your name here)
for successfully finishing this book.

 You're a star!

Multiplying and dividing

Write the answer in the box.

26 x 10 = $\boxed{260}$ 26 x 100 = $\boxed{2\,600}$

431 ÷ 10 = $\boxed{43.1}$ 431 ÷ 100 = $\boxed{4.31}$

Write the answer in the box.

33 x 10 = ___   21 x 10 = ___   42 x 10 = ___

94 x 100 = ___   36 x 100 = ___   81 x 100 = ___

416 x 10 = ___   204 x 10 = ___   513 x 10 = ___

767 x 100 = ___   821 x 100 = ___   245 x 100 = ___

Write the answer in the box.

127 ÷ 10 = ___   263 ÷ 10 = ___   471 ÷ 10 = ___

112 ÷ 100 = ___   844 ÷ 100 = ___   393 ÷ 100 = ___

25 ÷ 10 = ___   32 ÷ 10 = ___   27 ÷ 10 = ___

51 ÷ 100 = ___   22 ÷ 100 = ___   94 ÷ 100 = ___

Find the number that has been multiplied by 100.

___ x 100 = 5 900   ___ x 100 = 71 400

___ x 100 = 72 100   ___ x 100 = 23 400

___ x 100 = 1 100   ___ x 100 = 47 000

___ x 100 = 8 400   ___ x 100 = 44 100

Find the number that has been divided by 100.

___ ÷ 100 = 3.64   ___ ÷ 100 = 8.5

___ ÷ 100 = 21.37   ___ ÷ 100 = 18.2

___ ÷ 100 = 86.43   ___ ÷ 100 = 21

___ ÷ 100 = 1.05   ___ ÷ 100 = 5.92

Ordering sets of amounts

Write these amounts in order, starting with the smallest.

70 cm	300 mm	2 km	6 m	500 mm
300 mm	*500 mm*	*70 cm*	*6 m*	*2 km*

Write these amounts in order, starting with the smallest.

500p	£4.00	£5.50	350p	640p

2 kg	750 g	1500 g	1.6 kg	300 g

125 min	2 hours	$3\frac{1}{2}$ hours	200 min	$\frac{3}{4}$ hour

2 500 m	2 km	1 000 cm	20 m	1 000 m

£240	3 500p	£125.00	4 600p	£50.00

400 mm	60 cm	12 cm	0.5 m	1 km

0.75 kg	500 g	1 kg	300 g	900 g

2 hours	75 min	$1\frac{1}{2}$ hours	100 min	150 min

44 mm	4 cm	4 m	4 km	40 cm

1 200 m	1 km	750 m	0.5 km	200 m

Calculating temperature rise and fall

The temperature at midnight was –6°C.
By midday it was 4°C. By how much had
the temperature increased?

10°C

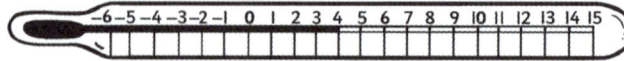

What is the difference in temperature between:

–2°C and 7°C

–1°C and 7°C

–7°C and 10°C

–9°C and –1°C

–12°C and 0°C

–3°C and 6°C

–21°C and 13°C

–5°C and 10°C

–4°C and 2°C

–8°C and 5°C

–11°C and 5°C

–4°C and 7°C

–15°C and 21°C

–19°C and 12°C

Write the answer in the box.

The temperature in Moscow is –5°C. If it rises to 3°C,
by how much has it risen?

The temperature in London is 18°C. If it rises to 25°C,
by how much has it risen?

The temperature in Bangkok is 29°C. The temperature in
Chicago is –3°C. How much warmer than Chicago is Bangkok?

The temperature at 7 a.m. is –3°C. At noon it is 7°C. By how
much has it risen?

The thermometer in a garage reads 8°C. If it has risen 11°C since
6 a.m., what was the temperature then?

The temperature inside a house is 17°C. Outside it is –4°C.
How much warmer is it inside than outside?

Counting in constant steps

Continue each row.

Steps of 3

$-2\frac{1}{2}$	$\frac{1}{2}$	$3\frac{1}{2}$	$6\frac{1}{2}$	$9\frac{1}{2}$	$12\frac{1}{2}$

Steps of 5

3.5	-1.5	-6.5	-11.5	-16.5	-21.5

Continue each row.

$-15\frac{1}{2}$	$-10\frac{1}{2}$	$-5\frac{1}{2}$			
$-5\frac{1}{4}$	$-3\frac{1}{4}$	$-1\frac{1}{4}$			
$-8\frac{1}{3}$	$-7\frac{1}{3}$	$-6\frac{1}{3}$		$-4\frac{1}{3}$	
$5\frac{1}{4}$	$-4\frac{3}{4}$	$-14\frac{3}{4}$			
$12\frac{1}{2}$	$8\frac{1}{2}$	$4\frac{1}{2}$			$-7\frac{1}{2}$
7.5	5.5	3.5			
9.4	5.4	1.4		-6.6	
11.6	3.6	-4.4			
-6.3	-2.3	1.7			
-12.1	-7.1	-2.1			12.9
-14.6	-7.6	-0.6			
$1\frac{1}{2}$	$-3\frac{1}{2}$	$-8\frac{1}{2}$			
-8.4	-5.4	-2.4		3.6	
$-7\frac{1}{4}$	$-1\frac{1}{4}$	$4\frac{3}{4}$			$22\frac{3}{4}$
7.5	-1.5	-10.5			

Reading and writing numbers

264 346 in words is Two hundred and sixty-four thousand, three hundred and forty-six

One million, three hundred and twelve thousand, five hundred and two is 1 312 502

Write each of these numbers in words.

326 208

704 543

240 701

278 520

Write each of these in numbers.

Five hundred and seventeen thousand and forty-two

Six hundred and ninety-four thousand, seven hundred and eleven

Eight hundred and nine thousand, two hundred and three

Nine hundred thousand, four hundred and four

Write each of these in numbers.

9 307 012

5 042 390

9 908 434

8 400 642

Write each of these in numbers.

Eight million, two hundred and fifty-one

Two million, forty thousand, four hundred and four

Seven million, three hundred and two thousand, one hundred and one

Two million, five hundred and forty-one thousand and five

Squares of numbers

Find the square of 2.

$$2 \times 2 = 4$$

What is the area of this square?

2 cm

2 cm

$$2 \times 2 = 4$$
area = 4 cm²

Find the square of these numbers.

3   1   6

7   8   5

9   4   10

Now try these.

13   20   40

11   12   30

What are the areas of these squares?

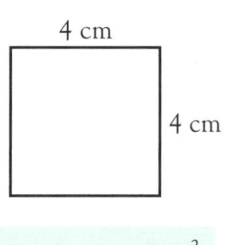
4 cm
4 cm

cm²

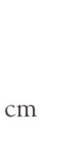
5 cm
5 cm

cm²

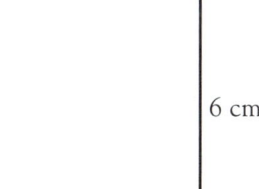
6 cm
6 cm

cm²

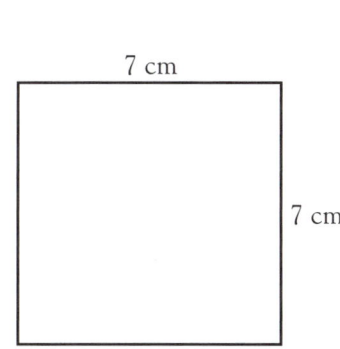
7 cm
7 cm

cm²

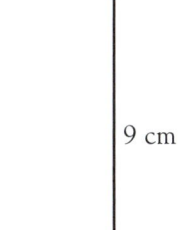
9 cm
9 cm

cm²

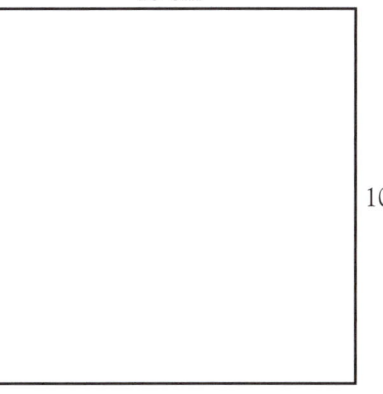
10 cm
10 cm

cm²

The factors of 66 are   1   2   3   6   11   22   33   66

Circle the factors of 94. (1) (2) (47)   28   32 (94)   86   43   71

Write the factors of each number in the box.

The factors of 70 are

The factors of 85 are

The factors of 69 are

The factors of 83 are

The factors of 75 are

The factors of 96 are

The factors of 63 are

The factors of 99 are

The factors of 72 are

Circle the factors of 68.

   1   2   3   4   5   6   7   8   9   11   12   17   34   35   62   68

Circle the factors of 95.

   1   2   3   4   5   15   16   17   19   24   37   85   90   95   96

Circle the factors of 88.

   1   2   3   4   5   6   8   10   11   15   22   25   27   44   87   88

Circle the factors of 73.

   1   2   4   5   6   8   9   10   12   13   14   15   30   60   73

Some numbers only have factors of 1 and themselves. They are called prime numbers. Write down all the prime numbers between 66 and 100 in the box.

Changing improper fractions to mixed numbers

Change this improper fraction to a mixed number in its simplest form.

$$\frac{27}{12} = 2\frac{3}{12} = 2\frac{1}{4}$$

Change these mixed numbers to top-heavy fractions.

$$2\frac{3}{4} = \frac{11}{4} \qquad\qquad 4\frac{1}{2} = \frac{9}{2}$$

Change these top-heavy fractions to mixed numbers.

$\frac{25}{3} =$ 　　　　　$\frac{15}{12} =$ 　　　　　$\frac{40}{7} =$

$\frac{17}{6} =$ 　　　　　$\frac{11}{9} =$ 　　　　　$\frac{12}{5} =$

$\frac{27}{5} =$ 　　　　　$\frac{26}{3} =$ 　　　　　$\frac{32}{5} =$

$\frac{9}{2} =$ 　　　　　$\frac{19}{2} =$ 　　　　　$\frac{15}{4} =$

$\frac{30}{4} =$ 　　　　　$\frac{26}{8} =$ 　　　　　$\frac{42}{9} =$

Change these mixed numbers to top-heavy fractions.

$4\frac{3}{4} =$ 　　　　　$9\frac{1}{2} =$ 　　　　　$12\frac{1}{4} =$

$3\frac{2}{3} =$ 　　　　　$6\frac{3}{4} =$ 　　　　　$3\frac{9}{10} =$

$5\frac{1}{8} =$ 　　　　　$3\frac{2}{5} =$ 　　　　　$2\frac{5}{6} =$

$5\frac{1}{4} =$ 　　　　　$3\frac{3}{8} =$ 　　　　　$2\frac{11}{12} =$

$2\frac{7}{10} =$ 　　　　　$4\frac{3}{10} =$ 　　　　　$4\frac{1}{8} =$

$7\frac{3}{4} =$ 　　　　　$8\frac{1}{2} =$ 　　　　　$1\frac{5}{12} =$

Ordering sets of decimals

Write these decimals in order starting with the smallest.

5.63	2.14	5.6	3.91	1.25	4.63
9.39	0.24	7.63	8.25	7.49	9.40
1.05	2.36	1.09	2.41	7.94	1.50
3.92	5.63	2.29	4.62	5.36	2.15
28.71	21.87	27.18	21.78	28.17	27.81

Write these amounts in order starting with the smallest.

£56.25	£32.40	£11.36	£32.04	£55.26	£36.19
94.21 km	87.05 km	76.91 km	94.36 km	65.99 km	110.75 km
26.41 kg	47.23 kg	26.14 kg	35.23 kg	49.14 kg	35.32 kg
19.51 m	16.15 m	15.53 m	12.65 m	24.24 m	16.51 m
7.35 l	8.29 l	5.73 l	8.92 l	10.65 l	4.29 l

Percentages as fractions of 100

Write these fractions as percentages.

$$\frac{7}{10} = \quad 70\%$$

$$\frac{1}{5} = \quad 20\%$$

Write this percentage as a fraction.

$$65\% = \frac{\overset{13}{\cancel{65}}}{\underset{20}{\cancel{100}}} = \frac{13}{20}$$

Write these fractions as percentages.

$$\frac{2}{5} = \qquad \qquad \frac{3}{10} = \qquad \qquad \frac{1}{2} =$$

$$\frac{9}{10} = \qquad \qquad \frac{3}{5} = \qquad \qquad \frac{4}{5} =$$

$$\frac{1}{10} = \qquad \qquad \frac{1}{4} = \qquad \qquad \frac{3}{4} =$$

Now try these.

$$\frac{3}{100} = \qquad \qquad \frac{7}{100} = \qquad \qquad \frac{9}{100} =$$

$$\frac{23}{100} = \qquad \qquad \frac{47}{100} = \qquad \qquad \frac{93}{100} =$$

Change these percentages to fractions. Remember that you may need to simplify.

20% =   45% =   55% =

12% =   35% =   60% =

Work out the answer to each calculation.
Cyril ate $\frac{2}{5}$ of a box of chocolates.
What percentage did he have left?

Tasmin put a 10% deposit on a dress in the sale. What fraction of the price did she still have to pay?

11

Working out percentages

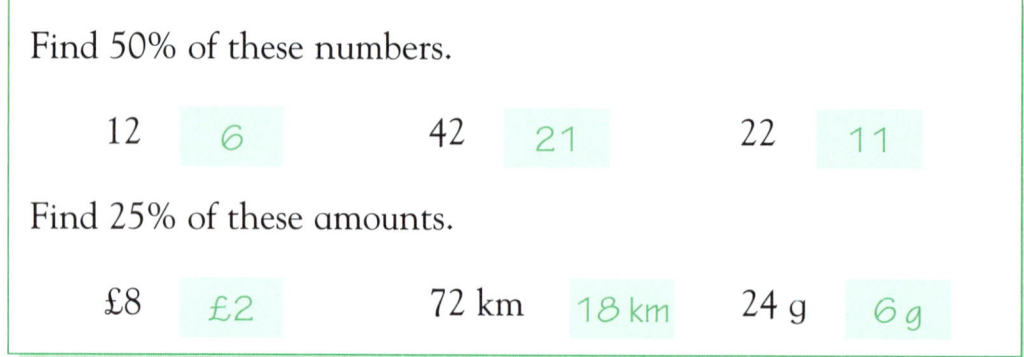

Find 50% of these numbers.

| 12 | 6 | 42 | 21 | 22 | 11 |

Find 25% of these amounts.

| £8 | £2 | 72 km | 18 km | 24 g | 6 g |

Find 50% of these numbers.

| 68 | | 46 | | 18 | |
| 36 | | 100 | | 80 | |

Find 25% of these numbers.

| 12 | | 48 | | 36 | |
| 20 | | 4 | | 40 | |

Find 75% of these amounts.

| £28.00 | | 12 cm | | 100 l | |
| 44 km | | £60.00 | | 16 m | |

Find 10% of these amounts.

£200.00		70 m		30 cm	
24 l		£37.00		48 g	
62 km		27 cm		36 l	

Write the answer in the box.

25% of a number is 12. What is the number?

10% of a number is 14. What is the number?

Mark spent 25% of his money. If he still has £60, how much did he spend?

Adding numbers in longer lists

Work out the answers to these sums.

£327	1 374 km
£644	2 362 km
£923	1 690 km
+ £455	+ 4 216 km
£2 349	**9 642 km**
2 1 1	1 2 1

Work out the answers to these sums.

539 m	206 m	481 m	735 m
965 m	812 m	604 m	234 m
774 m	619 m	274 m	391 m
+ 347 m	+ 832 m	+ 976 m	+ 863 m
m	m	m	m

746 kg	817 kg	944 kg	763 kg
201 kg	591 kg	835 kg	861 kg
432 kg	685 kg	391 kg	608 kg
+ 309 kg	+ 245 kg	+ 105 kg	+ 671 kg
kg	kg	kg	kg

6 329 m	5 245 m	6 431 m	8 690 m
3 251 m	2 845 m	7 453 m	5 243 m
2 642 m	1 937 m	4 650 m	6 137 m
+ 4 823 m	+ 5 610 m	+ 3 782 m	+ 5 843 m
m	m	m	m

£4 721	£3 654	£8 172	£4 352
£1 711	£5 932	£1 475	£3 920
£8 342	£6 841	£7 760	£8 439
+ £2 365	+ £4 736	+ £8 102	+ £1 348
£	£	£	£

1 573 km	4 902 km	3 756 km	8 010 km
6 231 km	7 547 km	1 150 km	7 793 km
2 112 km	8 463 km	5 535 km	1 641 km
+ 2 141 km	+ 6 418 km	+ 3 852 km	+ 7 684 km
km	km	km	km

Adding numbers in longer lists

Work out the answers to these sums.

3 461 km	£3 645
2 100 km	£4 231
3 522 km	£8 560
4 159 km	£7 213
+ 3 614 km	+ £9 463
16 856 km	£33 112
1 11	2 21

Work out the answers to these sums.

3 144 m	2 510 m	3 276 m	1 475 m
2 345 m	1 734 m	1 593 m	2 653 m
8 479 m	5 421 m	6 837 m	2 765 m
1 004 m	3 205 m	1 769 m	3 742 m
+ 6 310 m	+ 2 365 m	+ 3 846 m	+5 905 m
m	m	m	m

£1 480	£4 527	£3 063	£8 741
£6 366	£8 309	£8 460	£6 334
£1 313	£6 235	£2 712	£3 231
£3 389	£4 487	£3 756	£6 063
+ £4 592	+ £4 065	+ £5 650	+ £4 096
£	£	£	£

8 644 km	3 823 km	8 636 km	8 618 km
3 353 km	9 275 km	8 986 km	3 453 km
6 400 km	3 669 km	5 367 km	4 404 km
5 768 km	2 998 km	6 863 km	4 361 km
+ 1 092 km	+ 7 564 km	+ 3 605 km	+5 641 km
km	km	km	km

£3 742	£8 596	£2 739	£8 463
£2 785	£5 430	£6 517	£5 641
£7 326	£8 379	£6 014	£9 430
£1 652	£2 943	£7 115	£8 204
+ £5 753	+ £1 081	+ £2 704	+ £6 326
£	£	£	£

Rounding numbers

Write these numbers to the nearest 10.

24 is		91 is		55 is		73 is	
57 is		68 is		49 is		35 is	
82 is		37 is		22 is		52 is	
46 is		26 is		85 is		99 is	
43 is		51 is		78 is		29 is	

Write these numbers to the nearest 100.

386 is		224 is		825 is		460 is	
539 is		429 is		378 is		937 is	
772 is		255 is		549 is		612 is	
116 is		750 is		618 is		990 is	
940 is		843 is		172 is		868 is	

Write these numbers to the nearest 1 000.

3 240 is		2 500 is		9 940 is		1 051 is	
8 945 is		5 050 is		5 530 is		4 850 is	
6 200 is		7 250 is		8 499 is		8 450 is	
12 501 is		8 762 is		6 500 is		3 292 is	
1 499 is		14 836 is		10 650 is		11 241 is	

Rounding decimals

Write these decimals to the nearest tenth.

6.23 is   6.2   6.27 is   6.3

If the second decimal place is a 5, we round up the first decimal place to the number above.

6.25 is   6.3

Write these decimals to the nearest tenth.

9.21 is	4.38 is	2.47 is
3.48 is	8.17 is	6.28 is
7.14 is	3.91 is	2.56 is
8.41 is	2.36 is	1.53 is

Write these decimals to the nearest tenth.

9.35 is	8.71 is	6.05 is
1.19 is	3.65 is	4.21 is
8.55 is	7.35 is	9.14 is
6.83 is	2.15 is	6.34 is

Write these decimals to the nearest tenth.

25.61 is	14.35 is	11.24 is
16.85 is	24.34 is	71.36 is
26.85 is	11.54 is	37.25 is
92.42 is	95.65 is	27.36 is
45.17 is	36.75 is	22.05 is

Adding decimal fractions

Write the answer to each sum.

$$\begin{array}{r} £36.38 \\ +£22.05 \\ \hline £58.43 \\ \hline 1 \end{array}$$

$$\begin{array}{r} 27.46 \text{ m} \\ +\ 15.81 \text{ m} \\ \hline 43.27 \text{ m} \\ \hline 1\ 1 \end{array}$$

Write the answer to each sum.

$$\begin{array}{r} £14.61 \\ +£35.14 \\ \hline \end{array}$$
$$\begin{array}{r} £29.13 \\ +£62.75 \\ \hline \end{array}$$
$$\begin{array}{r} £34.71 \\ +£25.78 \\ \hline \end{array}$$

$$\begin{array}{r} £26.75 \\ +£85.43 \\ \hline \end{array}$$
$$\begin{array}{r} £15.89 \\ +£79.15 \\ \hline \end{array}$$
$$\begin{array}{r} £43.65 \\ +£35.10 \\ \hline \end{array}$$

$$\begin{array}{r} 17.58 \text{ m} \\ +65.77 \text{ m} \\ \hline \end{array}$$
$$\begin{array}{r} 45.83 \text{ m} \\ +38.21 \text{ m} \\ \hline \end{array}$$
$$\begin{array}{r} 29.98 \text{ m} \\ +72.35 \text{ m} \\ \hline \end{array}$$

$$\begin{array}{r} 43.87 \text{ m} \\ +51.97 \text{ m} \\ \hline \end{array}$$
$$\begin{array}{r} 76.92 \text{ m} \\ +31.88 \text{ m} \\ \hline \end{array}$$
$$\begin{array}{r} 64.83 \text{ m} \\ +27.93 \text{ m} \\ \hline \end{array}$$

Write the answer to each sum in the box.

£23.79 + £44.68 =

£52.97 + £84.29 =

£67.29 + £44.82 =

£77.38 + £49.82 =

Work out the answer to each sum.

Sean buys a computer game for £65.99.
He already has one that cost £52.45.
How much has he spent on computer games?

Mrs Kapur's car holds 42.57 litres of petrol.
Her husband's car holds 63.41 litres of petrol.
How much petrol must they buy to fill both cars?

Adding decimal fractions

Write the answer to each sum.

£73.24	84.61 m
+£16.99	+ 13.98 m
£90.23	98.59 m
1 1	1

Write the answer to each sum.

£28.77	£13.65	£28.99
+£45.45	+ £37.66	+ £34.93

£17.79	£20.58	£39.76
+£74.33	+ £69.55	+ £24.34

18.48 m	23.95 m	17.68 m
+ 34.93 m	+ 27.15 m	+16.27 m

84.64 m	23.29 m	73.81 m
+ 16.38 m	+ 36.82 m	+26.89 m

Write the answer to each sum in the box.

£64.82 + £39.28 =

£97.47 + £29.34 =

£32.91 + £11.39 =

£52.63 + £18.57 =

Work out the answer to each sum.

A family's shopping comes to £67.48 the first week and £84.63 the following week. How much was spent over the two weeks?

A builder needs 47.32 metres of skirting for the downstairs of a house and 36.79 metres for the upstairs. How much skirting will he use?

Subtracting decimal fractions

Write the answer to each calculation.

$$
\begin{array}{r}
^{6}\!\!1\,1 \\
£27.\!\!2\!\!3 \\
-\ £14.46 \\
\hline
£12.77
\end{array}
\qquad\qquad
\begin{array}{r}
^{3}\!\!1\,1 \\
54.\!\!2\!\!1\ m \\
-\ 12.75\ m \\
\hline
41.46\ m
\end{array}
$$

Write the answer to each calculation.

$$
\begin{array}{r}
£93.52 \\
-\ £41.73 \\
\hline
\end{array}
\qquad
\begin{array}{r}
£79.24 \\
-\ £23.75 \\
\hline
\end{array}
\qquad
\begin{array}{r}
£82.63 \\
-\ £30.99 \\
\hline
\end{array}
$$

$$
\begin{array}{r}
£55.32 \\
-\ £11.54 \\
\hline
\end{array}
\qquad
\begin{array}{r}
£64.23 \\
-\ £20.57 \\
\hline
\end{array}
\qquad
\begin{array}{r}
£42.13 \\
-\ £10.26 \\
\hline
\end{array}
$$

$$
\begin{array}{r}
53.74\ m \\
-\ 21.76\ m \\
\hline
\end{array}
\qquad
\begin{array}{r}
68.26\ m \\
-\ 32.38\ m \\
\hline
\end{array}
\qquad
\begin{array}{r}
89.13\ m \\
-\ 34.35\ m \\
\hline
\end{array}
$$

$$
\begin{array}{r}
98.92\ m \\
-\ 42.83\ m \\
\hline
\end{array}
\qquad
\begin{array}{r}
74.61\ m \\
-\ 22.76\ m \\
\hline
\end{array}
\qquad
\begin{array}{r}
69.26\ m \\
-\ 25.99\ m \\
\hline
\end{array}
$$

Write the answer to each calculation in the box.

£64.31 – £41.32 =

£67.76 – £31.77 =

£93.18 – £31.99 =

£77.24 – £32.65 =

Work out the answer to each calculation.

Deepak has saved £97.63. He spends
£25.98. How much does he have left?

A roll of fabric has 95.43 metres on it. If
42.75 metres are sold, how much is left?

Subtracting decimal fractions

Write the answer to each calculation.

$$\begin{array}{r} {}^{7}\cancel{8}{}^{13}\cancel{4}{}^{15}\cancel{6}{}^{1}3 \\ \pounds 84.63 \\ -\pounds 54.64 \\ \hline \pounds 29.99 \end{array}$$

$$\begin{array}{r} {}^{8}\cancel{9}{}^{1}\cancel{3}{}^{2}\cancel{4}{}^{1}7\ \text{m} \\ 93.47\ \text{m} \\ -23.75\ \text{m} \\ \hline 69.72\ \text{m} \end{array}$$

Write the answer to each calculation.

£84.25	£63.78	£84.14
– £35.64	–£24.88	–£25.78

£94.56	£82.21	£33.21
– £35.57	–£22.48	–£13.37

62.11 m	43.15 m	97.12 m
– 11.96 m	– 12.26 m	–29.25 m

92.53 m	61.42 m	44.72 m
– 13.74 m	– 24.63 m	–19.84 m

Write the answer to each calculation in the box.

£72.31 – £33.59 =   £81.63 – £24.78 =

£81.32 – £24.99 =   £73.17 – £23.58 =

Work out the answer to each calculation.
Tracy's grandmother gives her £25.50.
If Tracy now has a total of £72.24,
how much did she have before?

A junior school child ran a race in 57.43 seconds. A secondary
school child ran the same race in 39.57 seconds. How much
faster was the secondary school child?

Multiplying by tens and units

Work out the answer to each calculation.

```
    56          45
  x 32        x 43
  1 680       1 800
     1           2
  1 1,2        1 35
      1           1
  1 792        1 935
```

Work out the answer to each calculation.

```
    56          23          47          84
  x 23        x 24        x 25        x 22
     0           0           0           0
```

```
    73          52          64          51
  x 34        x 35        x 33        x 32
     0           0           0           0
```

Work out the answer to each calculation.

```
    41          65          72          84
  x 62        x 54        x 68        x 71
```

```
    92          57          38          26
  x 63        x 82        x 94        x 75
```

     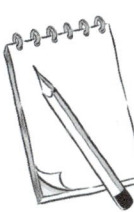

Multiplying by tens and units

Work out the answer to each calculation.

```
    39              68
  x 87            x 98
  ------          ------
  3 1,20          6 1,20
    7               7
    273             544
    6               6
  ------          ------
  3 393           6 664
```

Work out the answer to each calculation.

```
    87              76              99              85
  x 98            x 78            x 69            x 98
  ------          ------          ------          ------
       0               0               0               0
```

```
    88              67              94              89
  x 95            x 76            x 69            x 47
  ------          ------          ------          ------
       0               0               0               0
```

Work out the answer to each calculation.

```
    87              46              58              73
  x 79            x 67            x 59            x 98
  ------          ------          ------          ------
```

```
    95              58              78              96
  x 67            x 88            x 97            x 79
  ------          ------          ------          ------
```

   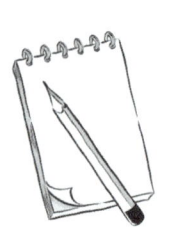  

Dividing by a single digit

Work out this calculation. Estimate your answer first.

257 divided by 3
There are roughly 30 3s in 100. 257 will be about $2\frac{1}{2}$ times
30 which equals 75. My answer should be near to 75.
$85\frac{2}{3}$ is about 10 away from my estimate, so my answer
is probably right.

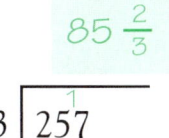

$$3\overline{)257}$$

Work out these calculations. Remember to estimate your answer first.

$2\overline{)571}$ $4\overline{)823}$ $3\overline{)604}$

$4\overline{)925}$ $2\overline{)147}$ $3\overline{)259}$

$4\overline{)839}$ $2\overline{)947}$ $3\overline{)502}$

Now try these.

$4\overline{)725}$ $2\overline{)811}$ $2\overline{)593}$

$4\overline{)406}$ $3\overline{)739}$ $4\overline{)591}$

$2\overline{)305}$ $5\overline{)263}$ $5\overline{)999}$

Write the answer in the box.

What is 319 divided
by 2?

What is 833 divided
by 3?

Dividing by a single digit

Work out this calculation. Estimate your answer first.

845 divided by 8.
There are roughly 100 8s in 800, and 45 is close to 8 x 5.
So my answer should be around 105.
$105\frac{5}{8}$ is very close to my estimate of 105.
My answer is probably right.

$$105\frac{5}{8}$$
$$8\overline{)8\,\overset{4}{4}5}$$

Work out these calculations. Remember to estimate your answer first.

$6\overline{)833}$ $7\overline{)465}$ $8\overline{)941}$

$9\overline{)812}$ $7\overline{)566}$ $7\overline{)499}$

$6\overline{)493}$ $6\overline{)247}$ $8\overline{)943}$

Now try these.

$8\overline{)532}$ $8\overline{)321}$ $7\overline{)635}$

$9\overline{)365}$ $6\overline{)598}$ $9\overline{)184}$

$7\overline{)212}$ $8\overline{)724}$ $9\overline{)112}$

Write the answer to each calculation in the box.

What is 553 divided by 6?

What is 924 divided by 8?

Real life problems

Work out the answer to each calculation.

Tim spends £26.54 on Christmas presents for his family. His sister spends £32.11. How much more does she spend than Tim?

£5.57

```
    2 1 1 1
£  3̶2̶.1̶1̶
-  £26.54
   £5.57
```

A school spends £99 per class on new books. If there are 16 classes in the school, how much is spent?

£1 584

```
    £99
  x  16
    990
   5,94
 £1 584
     1
```

Mr Brown has £4 762 in his building society and £2 247 in his bank. How much does he have altogether?

A shop in London takes £9 651 on a Saturday. A smaller branch in Portsmouth takes £3 247. How much more does the London shop take?

A school raises money for charity. If 127 children brought in £2 each and 261 children brought in £3 each, how much did they raise altogether?

David has to fill a pond that holds 250 l. If his bucket holds 4 l how many buckets of water will he need to fill the pond?

Samantha spends £14.25 on an aquarium, £3.75 on gravel, and £2.50 on aquarium ornaments. How much did she spend? How much change did she have from £25?

A man regularly saves £1 200 a year. How much will he save in 5 years?

Real life problems

Work out the answer to each calculation.

Ian runs round a field 8 times.
If he runs a total of 950 m,
what is the perimeter of the field?

$118\frac{3}{4}$ m

$118\frac{6\ 3}{8\ 4} = 118\frac{3}{4}$ m

$8\overline{)950}$ m

Mr and Mrs Green's lounge is 5.75 m long and their dining room is 4.37 m long.
If they knock out the wall between them to make one room, how long will it be?

10.12 m

```
  5.75 m
+ 4.37 m
_____
 10.12 m
   1 1
```

A family's journey took 5 hours. If they travelled at a steady speed of 50 kph, how far did they travel?

Two men weigh 87.43 kg and 92.12 kg.
What is the difference between their weights?

A builder uses 764 m of skirting board in 5 houses. If he uses the same amount in each, how much does he use per house?

A jar of coffee weighs 125 g.
How much will 7 jars weigh?

A box of pencils is 5 cm wide. How many can be stored on a shelf $\frac{1}{2}$ m long?

David spends 36 hours working on a school project. If he spreads the work evenly over 8 days, how many hours does he spend each day?

Sean runs 143.26 m in 40 seconds. Ivan runs 97.92 m in the same time. How much further does Sean run than Ivan?

Volumes of cubes and cuboids

This cube is 1 cm long, 1 cm high, and 1 cm wide.
We say it has a volume of 1 cubic cm (1 cm³).

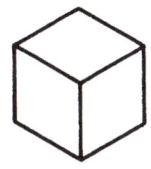 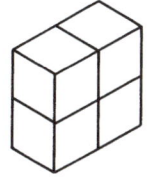

If we put 4 of these cubes together the new shape has a volume of 4 cm³.

These shapes are made of 1 cm³ cubes. What are their volumes?

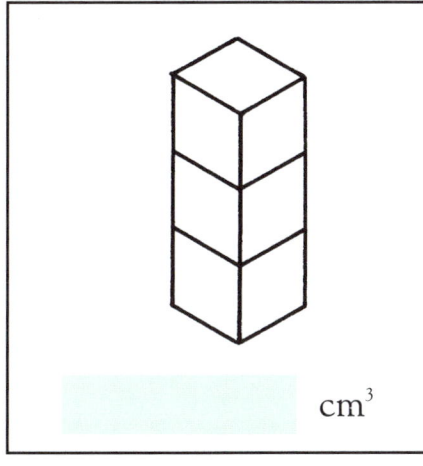

_____ cm³

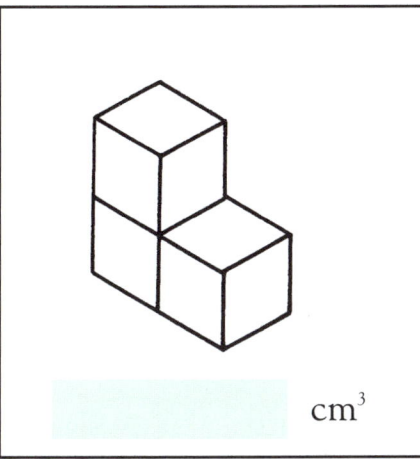

_____ cm³

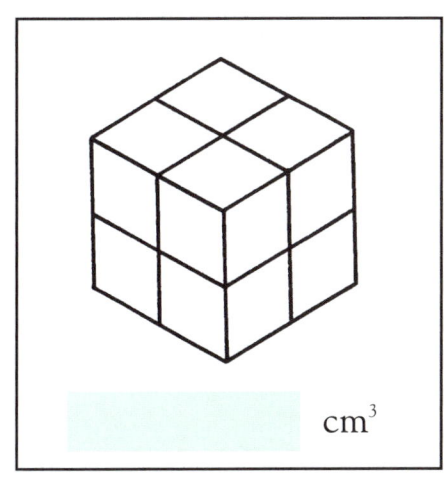

_____ cm³

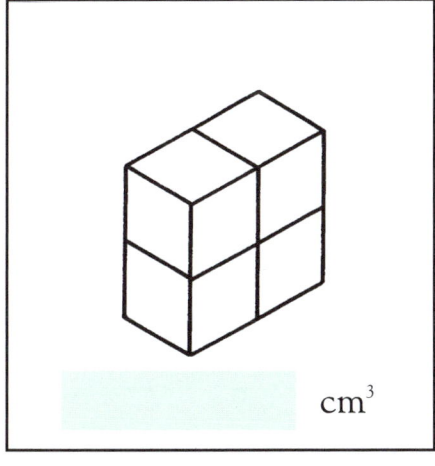

_____ cm³

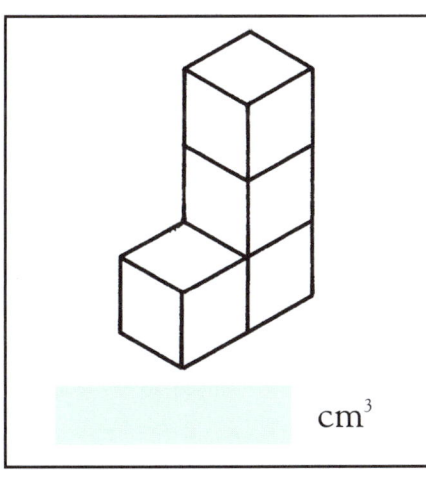

_____ cm³

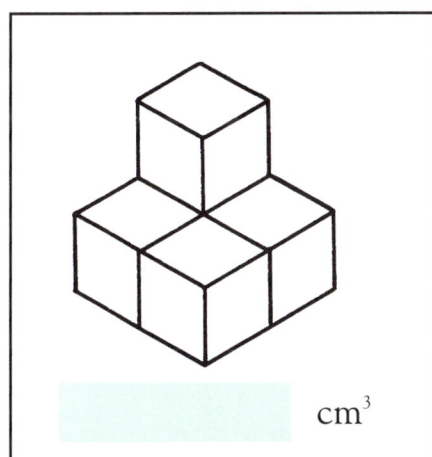

_____ cm³

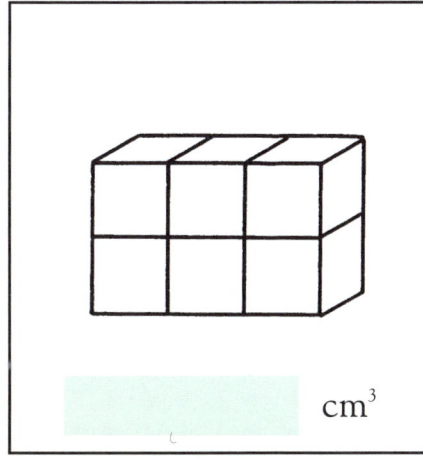

_____ cm³

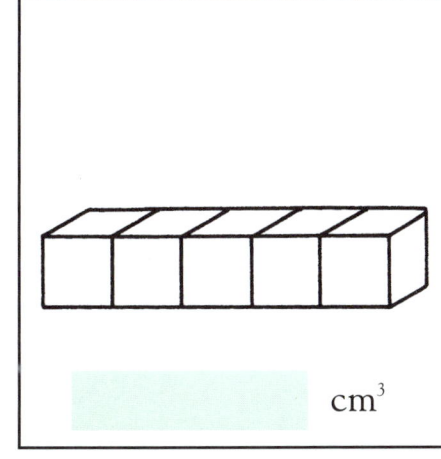

_____ cm³

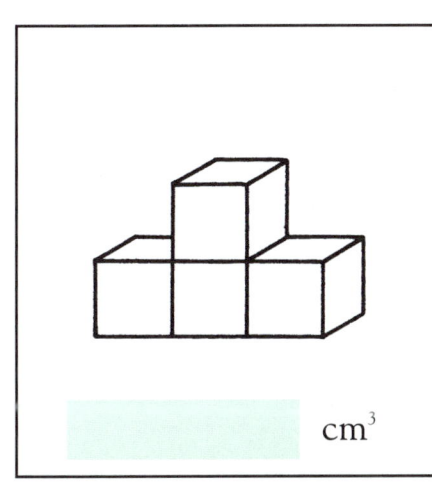

_____ cm³

Problems with time

Work out the answer to each calculation.

A car boot sale began at 09:15 and ended at 14:35. How long did it last?

$$
\begin{array}{r}
1\\
14:35\\
-09:15\\
\hline
5:20
\end{array}
$$

5 hours and 20 minutes

Fred's watch says 14:27. What time will it say in 1 hour 26 minutes?

$$
\begin{array}{r}
14:27\\
+\ \ 1:26\\
\hline
15:53\\
\scriptstyle 1
\end{array}
$$

15:53

Bret begins painting fence panels at 09:16 and finishes at 10:46. If he paints 3 fence panels, how long does each one take?

A team of 5 people works from 09:00 until 17:00 every day. If they each have an hour's lunch break, how many hours do they work altogether between Monday and Friday?

A train leaves at 08:47 and arrives at 16:29. How long does the journey take?

A castle has a 24-hour guard on the gate. Three soldiers share the work equally. If the first soldier starts his duty at 02:30, what time will the other two soldiers start their duties?

Soldier 2

Soldier 3

Courtney wants to videotape a programme that starts at 11:30 p.m. and finishes at 1:15 a.m. If the programme is on every night for the next five nights, how much video tape will he need?

Looking at graphs

Calvin records the temperature in his garden during one day.
At what time did the temperature reach its highest?   *noon*

By how much did the temperature fall between 6 p.m. and midnight?   *6° C*

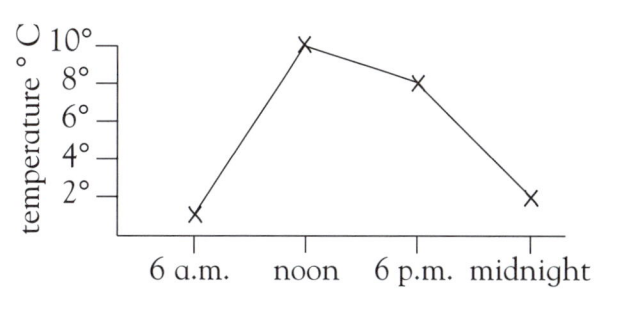

Bertie keeps a record of his last 10 spelling test results.

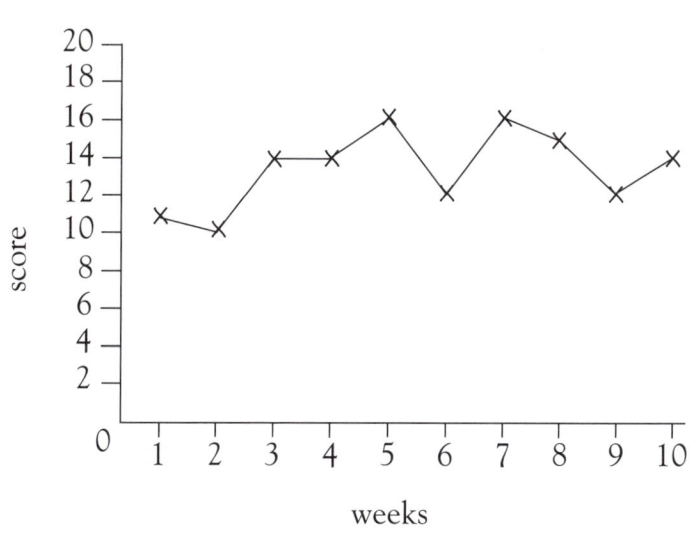

How many did Bertie get right in week 3?

Which 2 weeks running did Bertie's score stay the same?

What was Bertie's best score?

How much did his score improve between weeks 4 and 5?

The local tourist board has produced a graph to show the maximum temperatures in Eastend-on-Sea between April and August.

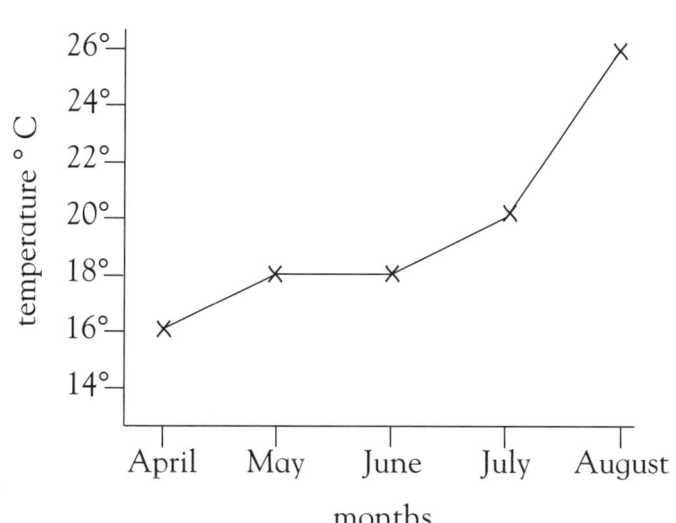

What was the maximum temperature in April?

Overall, what is happening to the temperature between April and August?

How much did the temperature rise between May and July?

Which two months had the same maximum temperature?

Area of basic compound shapes

Find the area of this shape.

To find the area of this shape we divide it into 2 rectangles and add the two areas together.

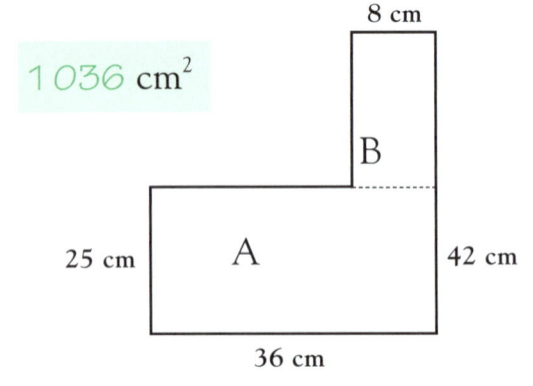

1036 cm²

8 cm

B

25 cm   A   42 cm

36 cm

```
A =  25           B = 17              900
   × 36                × 8        = + 136
    750         +      136 cm²       1036 cm²
    150                  5
    900 cm²
      1
```

Find the area of these shapes.

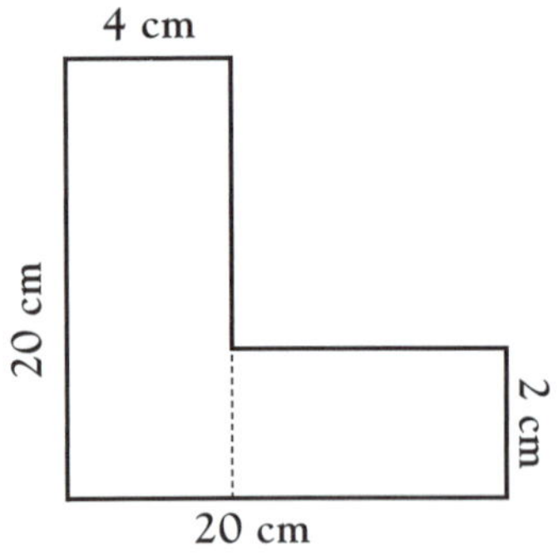

4 cm

20 cm

2 cm

20 cm

_____ cm²

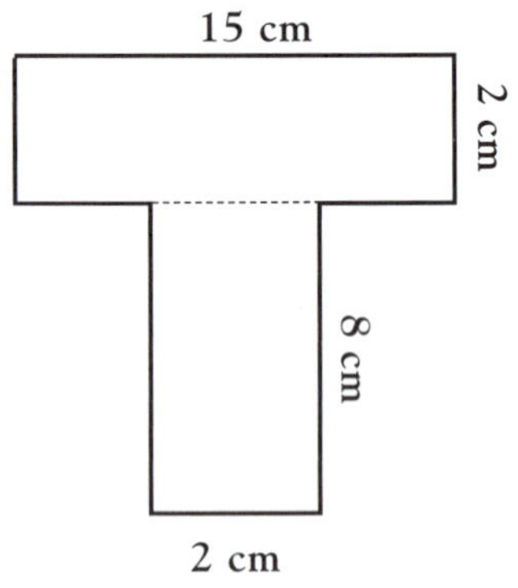

15 cm

2 cm

8 cm

2 cm

_____ cm²

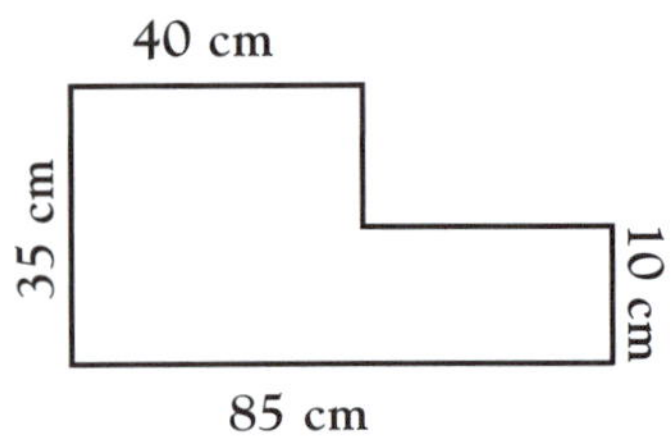

40 cm

35 cm

10 cm

85 cm

_____ cm²

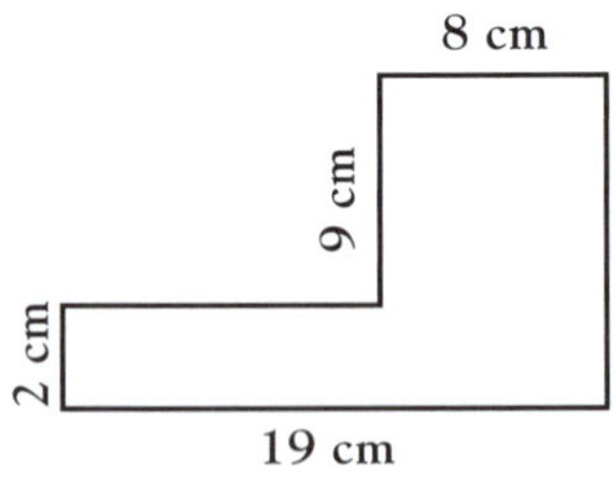

8 cm

9 cm

2 cm

19 cm

_____ cm²

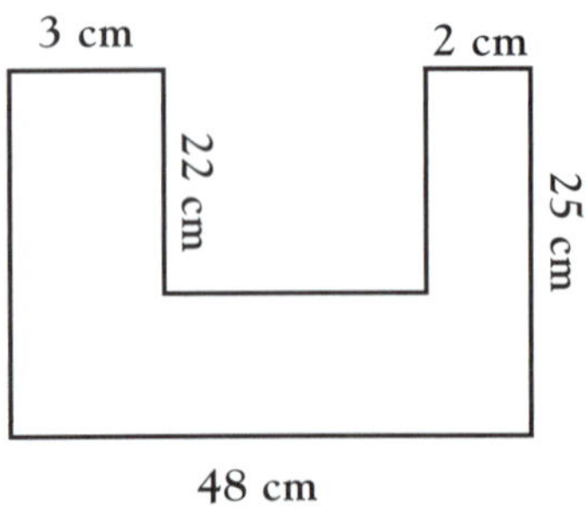

3 cm   2 cm

22 cm

25 cm

48 cm

_____ cm²

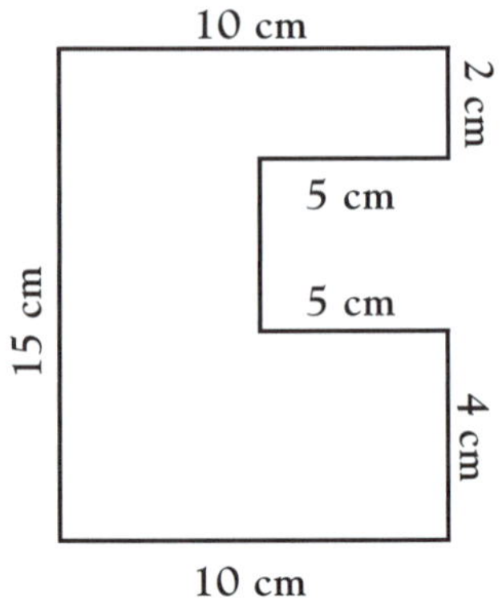

10 cm

2 cm

5 cm

5 cm

15 cm

4 cm

10 cm

_____ cm²

Area of basic compound shapes

Find the area of this shape.

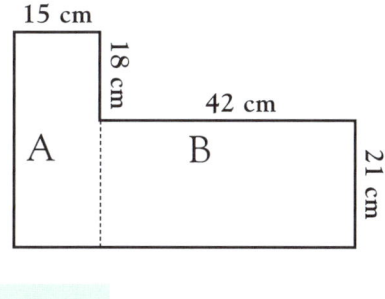

15 cm
18 cm
42 cm
A
B
21 cm

1 467 cm^2

To find the area of this shape we divide it into 2 rectangles and add the two areas together.

$$A = \begin{array}{r} 15 \\ \times\ 39 \\ \hline 450 \\ 135 \\ \hline 585 \text{ cm}^2 \end{array} \quad + \quad B = \begin{array}{r} 42 \\ \times\ 21 \\ \hline 840 \\ 42 \\ \hline 882 \text{ cm}^2 \end{array} \quad = \quad \begin{array}{r} 882 \\ +\ 585 \\ \hline 1\,467 \text{ cm}^2 \\ \hline 1 \end{array}$$

Find the area of each shape.

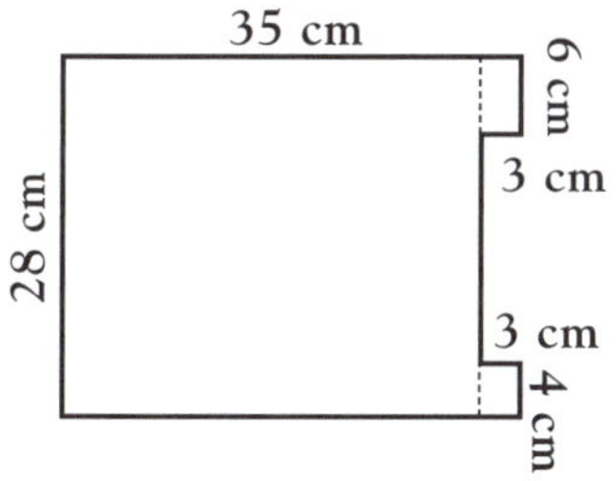

35 cm
6 cm
3 cm
28 cm
3 cm
4 cm

cm^2

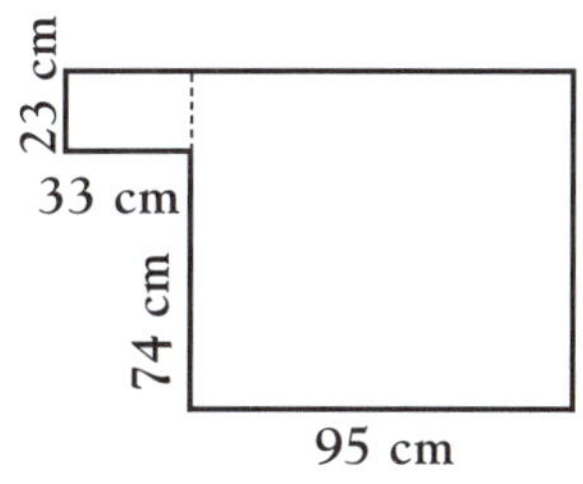

23 cm
33 cm
74 cm
95 cm

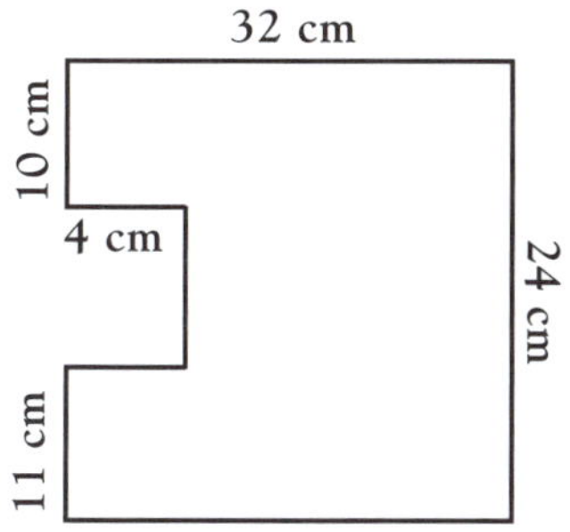

cm^2

32 cm
10 cm
4 cm
24 cm
11 cm

cm^2

45 cm
20 cm
14 cm
21 cm
21 cm
15 cm

cm^2

8 cm
9 cm
27 cm
24 cm
10 cm
26 cm

cm^2

98 cm
23 cm
25 cm
57 cm

cm^2

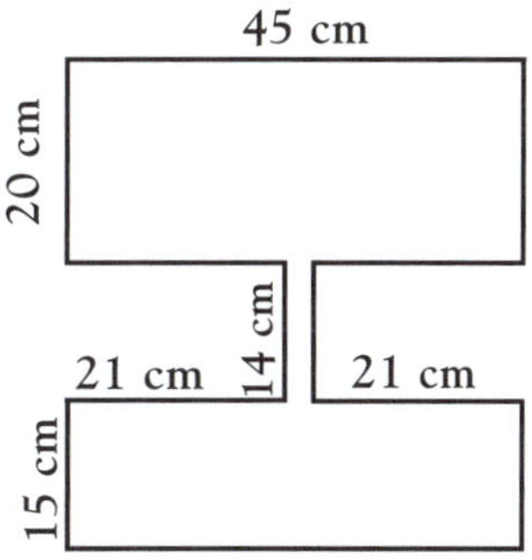

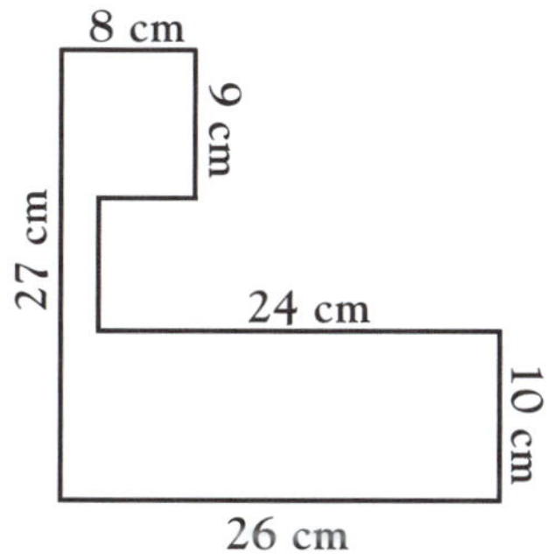

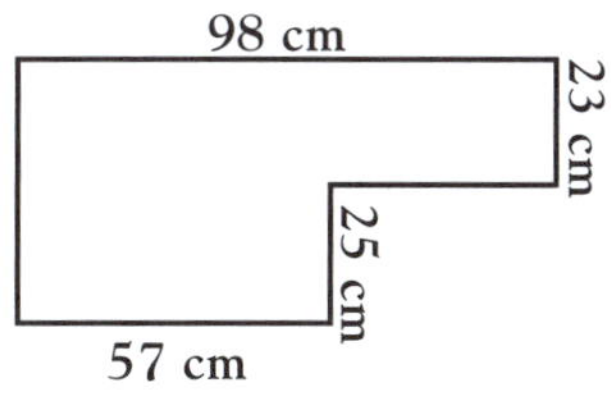

Acute and obtuse angles

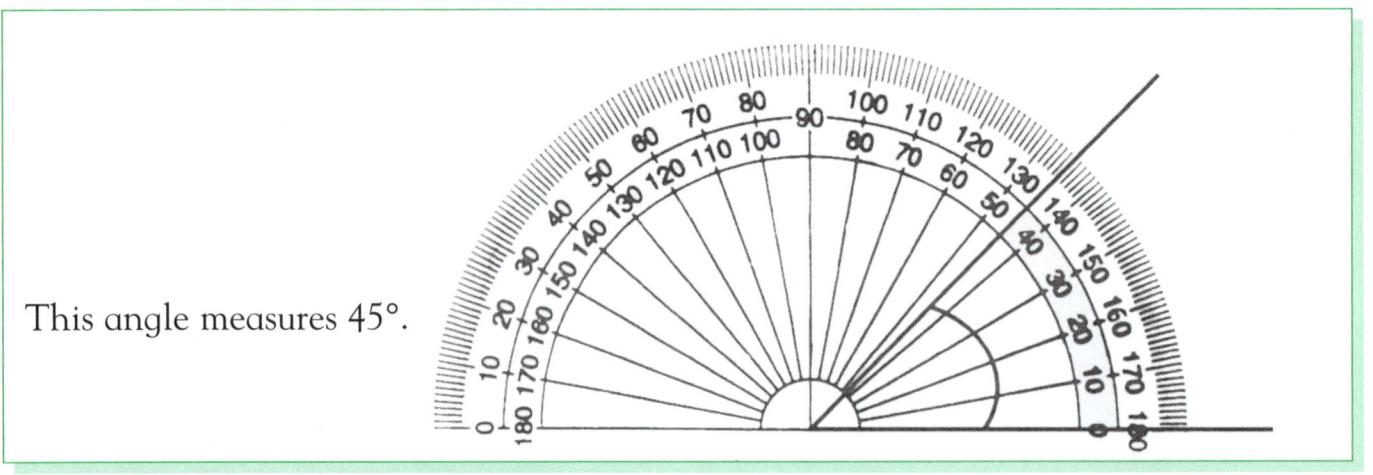

This angle measures 45°.

Use a protractor to measure these angles.

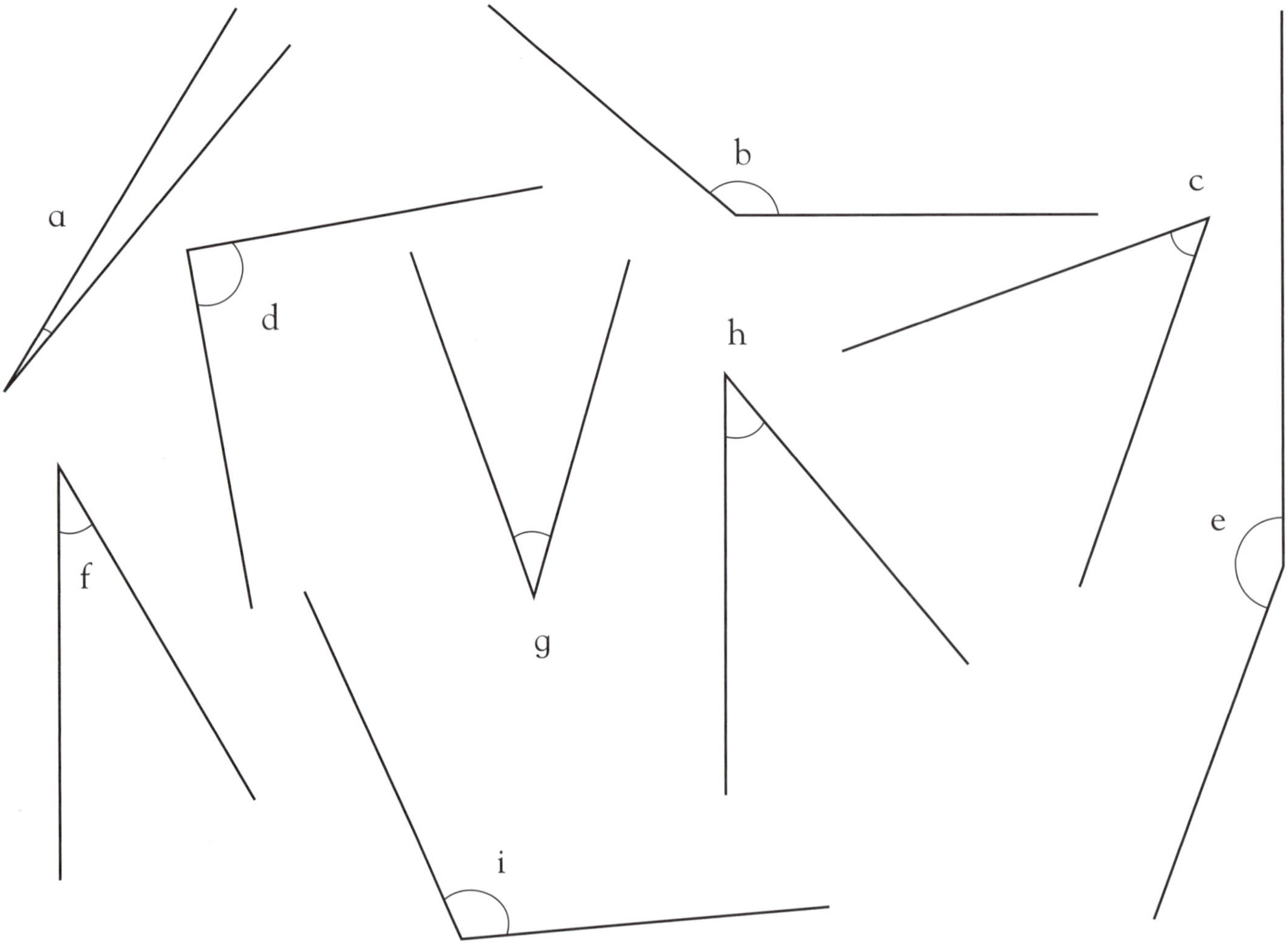

a

b

c

d

h

e

f

g

i

a	b	c	d

e	f	g	h

i

Answer Section with Parents' Notes

Key Stage 2
Ages 9–10
Advanced

This 8-page section provides answers to all the activities in the book. This will enable you to mark your children's work or can be used by them if they prefer to do their own marking.

The notes for each page help explain the common pitfalls and problems and, where appropriate, give indications as to what practice is needed to ensure your children understand where they have gone wrong.

⭐ Multiplying and dividing

Write the answer in the box.

| 26 x 10 = | 260 | 26 x 100 = | 2 600 |
| 431 ÷ 10 = | 43.1 | 431 ÷ 100 = | 4.31 |

Write the answer in the box.

33 x 10 = 330	21 x 10 = 210	42 x 10 = 420
94 x 100 = 9 400	36 x 100 = 3 600	81 x 100 = 8 100
416 x 10 = 4 160	204 x 10 = 2 040	513 x 10 = 5 130
767 x 100 = 76 700	821 x 100 = 82 100	245 x 100 = 24 500

Write the answer in the box.

127 ÷ 10 = 12.7	263 ÷ 10 = 26.3	471 ÷ 10 = 47.1
112 ÷ 100 = 1.12	844 ÷ 100 = 8.44	393 ÷ 100 = 3.93
25 ÷ 10 = 2.5	32 ÷ 10 = 3.2	27 ÷ 10 = 2.7
51 ÷ 100 = 0.51	22 ÷ 100 = 0.22	94 ÷ 100 = 0.94

Find the number that has been multiplied by 100.

59 x 100 = 5 900	714 x 100 = 71 400
721 x 100 = 72 100	234 x 100 = 23 400
11 x 100 = 1 100	470 x 100 = 47 000
84 x 100 = 8 400	441 x 100 = 44 100

Find the number that has been divided by 100.

364 ÷ 100 = 3.64	850 ÷ 100 = 8.5
2 137 ÷ 100 = 21.37	1 820 ÷ 100 = 18.2
8 643 ÷ 100 = 86.43	2 100 ÷ 100 = 21
105 ÷ 100 = 1.05	592 ÷ 100 = 5.92

Explain that multiplying by 10 or 100 means that the number becomes 10 times bigger (x10) or 100 times bigger (x100). In later sections, the inverse operation gives the number which has been operated on.

Ordering sets of amounts ⭐

Write these amounts in order, starting with the smallest.

| 70 cm | 300 mm | 2 km | 6 m | 500 mm |
| 300 mm | 500 mm | 70 cm | 6 m | 2 km |

Write these amounts in order, starting with the smallest.

| 500p | £4.00 | £5.50 | 350p | 640p |
| 350p | £4.00 | 500p | £5.50 | 640p |

| 2 kg | 750 g | 1500 g | 1.6 kg | 300 g |
| 300 g | 750 g | 1 500 g | 1.6 kg | 2 kg |

| 125 min | 2 hours | 3½ hours | 200 min | ¾ hour |
| ¾ hour | 2 hours | 125 min | 200 min | 3½ hours |

| 2 500 m | 2 km | 1 000 cm | 20 m | 1 000 m |
| 1 000 cm | 20 m | 1 000 m | 2 km | 2 500 m |

| £240 | 3 500p | £125.00 | 4 600p | £50.00 |
| 3 500p | 4 600p | £50.00 | £125.00 | £240 |

| 400 mm | 60 cm | 12 cm | 0.5 m | 1 km |
| 12 cm | 400 mm | 0.5 m | 60 cm | 1 km |

| 0.75 kg | 500 g | 1 kg | 300 g | 900 g |
| 300 g | 500 g | 0.75 kg | 900 g | 1 kg |

| 2 hours | 75 min | 1½ hours | 100 min | 150 min |
| 75 min | 1½ hours | 100 min | 2 hours | 150 min |

| 44 mm | 4 cm | 4 m | 4 km | 40 cm |
| 4 cm | 44 m | 40 cm | 4 m | 4 km |

| 1 200 m | 1 km | 750 m | 0.5 km | 200 m |
| 200 m | 0.5 km | 750 m | 1 km | 1 200 m |

The most likely problems on this page will stem from a lack of understanding of the relationship between amounts written in different ways. Look out for confusion between large amounts of small units and small amounts of large units, such as 350p and £4.00.

⭐ Calculating temperature rise and fall

The temperature at midnight was –6°C. By midday it was 4°C. By how much had the temperature increased? `10°C`

What is the difference in temperature between:

–2°C and 7°C	9°C	–5°C and 10°C	15°C
–1°C and 7°C	8°C	–4°C and 2°C	6°C
–7°C and 10°C	17°C	–8°C and 5°C	13°C
–9°C and –1°C	8°C	–11°C and 5°C	16°C
–12°C and 0°C	12°C	–4°C and 7°C	11°C
–3°C and 6°C	9°C	–15°C and 21°C	36°C
–21°C and 13°C	34°C	–19°C and 12°C	31°C

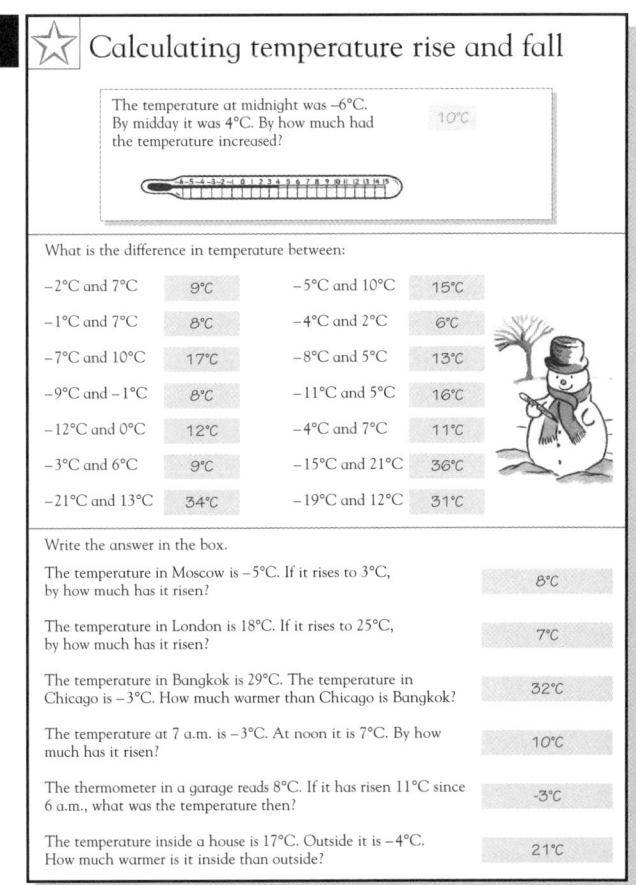

Write the answer in the box.

The temperature in Moscow is –5°C. If it rises to 3°C, by how much has it risen? `8°C`

The temperature in London is 18°C. If it rises to 25°C, by how much has it risen? `7°C`

The temperature in Bangkok is 29°C. The temperature in Chicago is –3°C. How much warmer than Chicago is Bangkok? `32°C`

The temperature at 7 a.m. is –3°C. At noon it is 7°C. By how much has it risen? `10°C`

The thermometer in a garage reads 8°C. If it has risen 11°C since 6 a.m., what was the temperature then? `-3°C`

The temperature inside a house is 17°C. Outside it is –4°C. How much warmer is it inside than outside? `21°C`

Watch out for children taking away the negative number from the positive; the difference between –2 and 7 may be wrongly calculated as 5. Use a number line that extends beyond 0 into negative numbers to show the difference.

5 Counting in constant steps

Continue each row.

Steps of 3

$-2\frac{1}{2}$	$\frac{1}{2}$	$3\frac{1}{2}$	$6\frac{1}{2}$	$9\frac{1}{2}$	$12\frac{1}{2}$

Steps of 5

3.5	−1.5	−6.5	−11.5	−16.5	−21.5

Continue each row.

$-15\frac{1}{2}$	$-10\frac{1}{2}$	$-5\frac{1}{2}$	$-\frac{1}{2}$	$4\frac{1}{2}$	$9\frac{1}{2}$
$-5\frac{1}{4}$	$-3\frac{1}{4}$	$-1\frac{1}{4}$	$\frac{3}{4}$	$2\frac{3}{4}$	$4\frac{3}{4}$
$-8\frac{1}{3}$	$-7\frac{1}{3}$	$-6\frac{1}{3}$	$-5\frac{1}{3}$	$-4\frac{1}{3}$	$-3\frac{1}{3}$
$5\frac{1}{4}$	$-4\frac{3}{4}$	$-14\frac{3}{4}$	$-24\frac{3}{4}$	$-34\frac{3}{4}$	$-44\frac{3}{4}$
$12\frac{1}{2}$	$8\frac{1}{2}$	$4\frac{1}{2}$	$\frac{1}{2}$	$-3\frac{1}{2}$	$-7\frac{1}{2}$
7.5	5.5	3.5	1.5	−0.5	−2.5
9.4	5.4	1.4	−2.6	−6.6	−10.6
11.6	3.6	−4.4	−12.4	−20.4	−28.4
−6.3	−2.3	1.7	5.7	9.7	13.7
−12.1	−7.1	−2.1	2.9	7.9	12.9
−14.6	−7.6	−0.6	6.4	13.4	20.4
$1\frac{1}{2}$	$-3\frac{1}{2}$	$-8\frac{1}{2}$	$-13\frac{1}{2}$	$-18\frac{1}{2}$	$-23\frac{1}{2}$
−8.4	−5.4	−2.4	0.6	3.6	6.6
$-7\frac{1}{4}$	$-1\frac{1}{4}$	$4\frac{3}{4}$	$10\frac{3}{4}$	$16\frac{3}{4}$	$22\frac{3}{4}$
7.5	−1.5	−10.5	−19.5	−28.5	−37.5

Point out that the steps can be found by taking the first number away from the second, the second from the third, and so on. Talk about the 'difference' between numbers, associating this word with subtraction. Be careful with fractions and decimals that cross zero.

6 Reading and writing numbers

264 346 in words is Two hundred and sixty-four thousand, three hundred and forty-six

One million, three hundred and twelve thousand, five hundred and two is 1 312 502

Write each of these numbers in words.

326 208	Three hundred and twenty-six thousand, two hundred and eight
704 543	Seven hundred and four thousand, five hundred and forty-three
240 701	Two hundred and forty thousand, seven hundred and one
278 520	Two hundred and seventy-eight thousand, five hundred and twenty

Write each of these in numbers.

Five hundred and seventeen thousand and forty-two	517 042
Six hundred and ninety-four thousand, seven hundred and eleven	694 711
Eight hundred and nine thousand, two hundred and three	809 203
Nine hundred thousand, four hundred and four	900 404

Write each of these in numbers.

9 307 012	Nine million, three hundred and seven thousand and twelve
5 042 390	Five million, forty-two thousand, three hundred and ninety
9 908 434	Nine million, nine hundred and eight thousand, four hundred and thirty-four
8 400 642	Eight million, four hundred thousand, six hundred and forty-two

Write each of these in numbers.

Eight million, two hundred and fifty-one	8 000 251
Two million, forty thousand, four hundred and four	2 040 404
Seven million, three hundred and two thousand, one hundred and one	7 302 101
Two million, five hundred and forty-one thousand and five	2 541 005

Children may miss the significance of zeroes and disregard them in their answers. Discuss this confusio[n] with place value carefully. Explain that when writing numbers in words they should not include the zeroes, e.g., eight thousand and twenty-four.

7 Squares of numbers

Find the square of 2. 2 x 2 = 4

What is the area of this square? 2 cm, 2 cm. 2 x 2 = 4, area = 4 cm²

Find the square of these numbers.

3	3 x 3 = 9	1	1 x 1 = 1	6	6 x 6 = 36
7	7 x 7 = 49	8	8 x 8 = 64	5	5 x 5 = 25
9	9 x 9 = 81	4	4 x 4 = 16	10	10 x 10 = 100

Now try these.

13	13 x 13 = 169	20	20 x 20 = 400	40	40 x 40 = 1600
11	11 x 11 = 121	12	12 x 12 = 144	30	30 x 30 = 900

What are the areas of these squares?

4 cm, 4 cm: 16 cm²

5 cm, 5 cm: 25 cm²

6 cm, 6 cm: 36 cm²

7 cm, 7 cm: 49 cm²

9 cm, 9 cm: 81 cm²

10 cm, 10 cm: 100 cm²

This page is fairly straightforward. However, check that the children are squaring the number and not multiplying it by two.

8 Factors of numbers from 66 to 100

The factors of 66 are 1 2 3 6 11 22 33 66

Circle the factors of 94. (1) (2) (47) 28 32 (94) 86 43 71

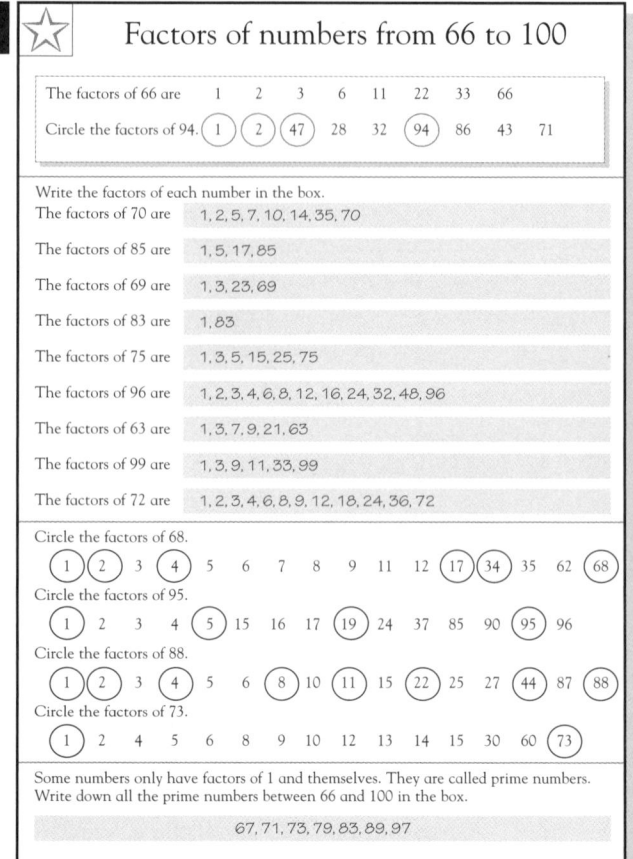

Write the factors of each number in the box.

The factors of 70 are	1, 2, 5, 7, 10, 14, 35, 70
The factors of 85 are	1, 5, 17, 85
The factors of 69 are	1, 3, 23, 69
The factors of 83 are	1, 83
The factors of 75 are	1, 3, 5, 15, 25, 75
The factors of 96 are	1, 2, 3, 4, 6, 8, 12, 16, 24, 32, 48, 96
The factors of 63 are	1, 3, 7, 9, 21, 63
The factors of 99 are	1, 3, 9, 11, 33, 99
The factors of 72 are	1, 2, 3, 4, 6, 8, 9, 12, 18, 24, 36, 72

Circle the factors of 68.

(1) (2) 3 (4) 5 6 7 8 9 11 12 (17) (34) 35 62 (68)

Circle the factors of 95.

(1) 2 3 4 (5) 15 16 17 (19) 24 37 85 90 (95) 96

Circle the factors of 88.

(1) (2) 3 (4) 5 6 (8) 10 (11) 15 (22) 25 27 (44) 87 (88)

Circle the factors of 73.

(1) 2 4 5 6 8 9 10 12 13 14 15 30 60 (73)

Some numbers only have factors of 1 and themselves. They are called prime numbers. Write down all the prime numbers between 66 and 100 in the box.

67, 71, 73, 79, 83, 89, 97

Quite often some factors of numbers get missed, especially as the numbers get larger. Encourage a systematic method of finding the factors. Children often forget that 1 and itself are factors of a number

Changing improper fractions to mixed numbers ☆

Change this improper fraction to a mixed number in its simplest form.

$$\frac{27}{12} = 2\frac{3}{12}^{1} = 2\frac{1}{4}$$

Change these mixed numbers to top-heavy fractions.

$$2\frac{3}{4} = \frac{11}{4} \qquad 4\frac{1}{2} = \frac{9}{2}$$

Change these top-heavy fractions to mixed numbers.

$\frac{25}{3} = 8\frac{1}{3}$	$\frac{15}{12} = 1\frac{1}{4}$	$\frac{40}{7} = 5\frac{5}{7}$
$\frac{17}{6} = 2\frac{5}{6}$	$\frac{11}{9} = 1\frac{2}{9}$	$\frac{12}{5} = 2\frac{2}{5}$
$\frac{27}{5} = 5\frac{2}{5}$	$\frac{26}{3} = 8\frac{2}{3}$	$\frac{32}{5} = 6\frac{2}{5}$
$\frac{9}{2} = 4\frac{1}{2}$	$\frac{19}{2} = 9\frac{1}{2}$	$\frac{15}{4} = 3\frac{3}{4}$
$\frac{30}{4} = 7\frac{1}{2}$	$\frac{26}{8} = 3\frac{1}{4}$	$\frac{42}{9} = 4\frac{2}{3}$

Change these mixed numbers to top-heavy fractions.

$4\frac{3}{4} = \frac{19}{4}$	$9\frac{1}{2} = \frac{19}{2}$	$12\frac{1}{4} = \frac{49}{4}$
$3\frac{2}{3} = \frac{11}{3}$	$6\frac{3}{4} = \frac{27}{4}$	$3\frac{9}{10} = \frac{39}{10}$
$5\frac{1}{8} = \frac{41}{8}$	$3\frac{2}{5} = \frac{17}{5}$	$2\frac{5}{6} = \frac{17}{6}$
$5\frac{1}{4} = \frac{21}{4}$	$3\frac{3}{8} = \frac{27}{8}$	$2\frac{11}{12} = \frac{35}{12}$
$2\frac{7}{10} = \frac{27}{10}$	$4\frac{3}{10} = \frac{43}{10}$	$4\frac{1}{8} = \frac{33}{8}$
$7\frac{3}{4} = \frac{31}{4}$	$8\frac{1}{2} = \frac{17}{2}$	$1\frac{5}{12} = \frac{17}{12}$

In the first part, the child should see that you can divide the denominator into the numerator and place the remainder over the denominator. Use card circles cut into equal parts to reinforce the idea, e.g., how many whole circles can you make from 17 quarter circles?

☆ Ordering sets of decimals

Write these decimals in order starting with the smallest.

0.45	0.21	2.07	1.45	3.62	2.17
0.21	0.45	1.45	2.07	2.17	3.62

Write these decimals in order starting with the smallest.

5.63	2.14	5.6	3.91	1.25	4.63
1.25	2.14	3.91	4.63	5.6	5.63
9.39	0.24	7.63	8.25	7.49	9.40
0.24	7.49	7.63	8.25	9.39	9.40
1.05	2.36	1.09	2.41	7.94	1.50
1.05	1.09	1.50	2.36	2.41	7.94
3.92	5.63	2.29	4.62	5.36	2.15
2.15	2.29	3.92	4.62	5.36	5.63
28.71	21.87	27.18	21.78	28.17	27.81
21.78	21.87	27.18	27.81	28.17	28.71

Write these amounts in order starting with the smallest.

£56.25	£32.40	£11.36	£32.04	£55.26	£36.19
£11.36	£32.04	£32.40	£36.19	£55.26	£56.25
94.21 km	87.05 km	76.91 km	94.36 km	65.99 km	110.75 km
65.99 km	76.91 km	87.05 km	94.21 km	94.36 km	110.75 km
26.41 kg	47.23 kg	26.14 kg	35.23 kg	49.14 kg	35.32 kg
26.14 kg	26.41 kg	35.23 kg	35.32 kg	47.23 kg	49.14 kg
19.51 m	16.15 m	15.53 m	12.65 m	24.24 m	16.51 m
12.65 m	15.53 m	16.15 m	16.51 m	19.51 m	24.24 m
7.35 l	8.29 l	5.73 l	8.92 l	10.65 l	4.29 l
4.29 l	5.73 l	7.35 l	8.29 l	8.92 l	10.65 l

Children should look at the units first. If there is more than one number with the same unit, look right to the tenths column for information necessary for sorting. Some numbers use similar digits but with different place values, therefore care is needed.

Percentages as fractions of 100 ☆

Write these fractions as percentages.

$$\frac{7}{10} = 70\% \qquad \frac{1}{5} = 20\%$$

Write this percentage as a fraction.

$$65\% = \frac{65}{100}^{13} = \frac{13}{20}$$

Write these fractions as percentages.

$\frac{2}{5} = 40\%$	$\frac{3}{10} = 30\%$	$\frac{1}{2} = 50\%$
$\frac{9}{10} = 90\%$	$\frac{3}{5} = 60\%$	$\frac{4}{5} = 80\%$
$\frac{1}{10} = 10\%$	$\frac{1}{4} = 25\%$	$\frac{3}{4} = 75\%$

Now try these.

$\frac{3}{100} = 3\%$	$\frac{7}{100} = 7\%$	$\frac{9}{100} = 9\%$
$\frac{23}{100} = 23\%$	$\frac{47}{100} = 47\%$	$\frac{93}{100} = 93\%$

Change these percentages to fractions. Remember that you may need to simplify.

$$20\% = \frac{20}{100}^{1}_{5} = \frac{1}{5} \qquad 45\% = \frac{45}{100}^{9}_{20} = \frac{9}{20} \qquad 55\% = \frac{55}{100}^{11}_{20} = \frac{11}{20}$$

$$12\% = \frac{12}{100}^{3}_{25} = \frac{3}{25} \qquad 35\% = \frac{35}{100}^{7}_{20} = \frac{7}{20} \qquad 60\% = \frac{60}{100}^{3}_{5} = \frac{3}{5}$$

Work out the answer to each calculation.

Cyril ate $\frac{2}{5}$ of a box of chocolates. What percentage did he have left?

60%

$$1 - \frac{2}{5} = \frac{3}{5}$$
$$\frac{3}{5} \times 100 = 60$$

Tasmin put a 10% deposit on a dress in the sale. What fraction of the price did she still have to pay?

$\frac{9}{10}$

$$100 - 10 = 90$$
$$\frac{90}{100} = \frac{9}{10}$$

Children may need help to see that if $\frac{1}{10}$ is the same as 10%, then $\frac{1}{5}$ is equal to 20% because it is $\frac{2}{10}$. You may have to remind them that 1% is equal to $\frac{1}{100}$. Any number divided by 100 will be the same as the percentage of that number.

☆ Working out percentages

Find 50% of these numbers.

12	6	42	21	22	11

Find 25% of these amounts.

£8	£2	72 km	18 km	24 g	6 g

Find 50% of these numbers.

68	34	46	23	18	9
36	18	100	50	80	40

Find 25% of these numbers.

12	3	48	12	36	9
20	5	4	1	40	10

Find 75% of these amounts.

£28.00	£21.00	12 cm	9 cm	100 l	75 l
44 km	33 km	£60.00	£45.00	16 m	12 m

Find 10% of these amounts.

£200.00	£20.00	70 m	7 m	30 cm	3 cm
24 l	2.4 l	£37.00	£3.70	48 g	4.8 g
62 km	6.2 km	27 cm	2.7 cm	36 l	3.6 l

Write the answer in the box.

25% of a number is 12. What is the number? — 48

10% of a number is 14. What is the number? — 140

Mark spent 25% of his money. If he still has £60, how much did he spend? — £20

Children should be aware that 50% is equal to $\frac{1}{2}$; 25% is equal to $\frac{1}{4}$; 75% is equal to $\frac{3}{4}$; and 10% is equal to $\frac{1}{10}$. They may convert units, e.g., 27 mm is 10% of 27 cm. This shows that they are comfortable with both conversion and percentage sums.

Adding numbers in longer lists ★

Work out the answers to these sums.

£327	1 374 km
£644	2 362 km
£923	1 690 km
+ £455	+ 4 216 km
£2 349	9 642 km
2 1 1	1 2 1

Work out the answers to these sums.

539 m	206 m	481 m	735 m
965 m	812 m	604 m	234 m
774 m	619 m	274 m	391 m
+ 347 m	+ 832 m	+ 976 m	+ 863 m
2 625 m	2 469 m	2 335 m	2 223 m
2 2	2 1	2 2	2 1

746 kg	817 kg	944 kg	763 kg
201 kg	591 kg	835 kg	861 kg
432 kg	685 kg	391 kg	608 kg
+ 309 kg	+ 245 kg	+ 105 kg	+ 671 kg
1 688 kg	2 338 kg	2 275 kg	2 903 kg
2 2	2 1	1	1

6 329 m	5 245 m	6 431 m	8 690 m
3 251 m	2 845 m	7 453 m	5 243 m
2 642 m	1 937 m	4 650 m	6 137 m
+ 4 823 m	+ 5 610 m	+ 3 782 m	+ 5 843 m
17 045 m	15 637 m	22 316 m	25 913 m
2 1 1	2 1	2 2	1 2 1

£4 721	£3 654	£8 172	£4 352
£1 711	£5 932	£1 475	£3 920
£8 342	£6 841	£7 760	£8 439
+ £2 365	+ £4 736	+ £8 102	+ £1 348
£ 17 139	£ 21 163	£ 25 509	£ 18 059
2 1	3 1 1	1 2	2 1

1 573 km	4 902 km	3 756 km	8 010 km
6 231 km	7 547 km	1 150 km	7 793 km
2 112 km	8 463 km	5 535 km	1 641 km
+ 2 141 km	+ 6 418 km	+ 3 852 km	+ 7 684 km
12 057 km	27 330 km	14 293 km	25 128 km
1 1	2 1 2	2 1 1	2 2

This page and the next should be fairly straightforward, but with larger lists involved there is always the possibility of errors creeping in. Look out for failure to exchange or forgetting to add on the numbers that have been exchanged.

★ Adding numbers in longer lists

Work out the answers to these sums.

3 461 km	£3 645
2 100 km	£4 231
3 522 km	£8 560
4 159 km	£7 213
+ 3 614 km	+ £9 463
16 856 km	£33 112
1 1	2 2 1

Work out the answers to these sums.

3 144 m	2 510 m	3 276 m	1 475 m
2 345 m	1 734 m	1 593 m	2 653 m
8 479 m	5 421 m	6 837 m	2 765 m
1 004 m	3 205 m	1 769 m	3 742 m
+ 6 310 m	+ 2 365 m	+ 3 846 m	+5 905 m
21 282 m	15 235 m	17 321 m	16 540 m
1 1 2	2 1 1	3 3 3	3 2 2

£1 480	£4 527	£3 063	£8 741
£6 366	£8 309	£8 460	£6 334
£1 313	£6 235	£2 712	£3 231
£3 389	£4 487	£3 756	£6 063
+ £4 592	+ £4 065	+ £5 650	+ £4 096
£17 140	£27 623	£23 641	£28 465
2 3 2	1 2 3	2 2 1	1 2 1

8 644 km	3 823 km	8 636 km	8 618 km
3 353 km	9 275 km	8 986 km	3 453 km
6 400 km	3 669 km	5 367 km	4 404 km
5 768 km	2 998 km	6 863 km	4 361 km
+ 1 092 km	+ 7 564 km	+ 3 605 km	+5 641 km
25 257 km	27 329 km	33 457 km	26 477 km
2 2 1	3 3 2	3 2 2	2 1 1

£3 742	£8 596	£2 739	£8 463
£2 785	£5 430	£6 517	£5 641
£7 326	£8 379	£6 014	£9 430
£1 652	£2 943	£7 115	£8 204
+ £5 753	+ £1 081	+ £2 704	+ £6 326
£21 258	£26 429	£ 25 089	£38 064
3 2 1	2 3 1	2 2	2 1 1

As with the previous page, problems may arise because of the long list of numbers.

Rounding numbers ★

Round these numbers up.

36 to the nearest 10	40
124 to the nearest 100	100
4 360 to the nearest 1 000	4 000

Remember if a number is half-way between it is rounded up.

Write these numbers to the nearest 10.

24 is	20	91 is	90	55 is	60	73 is	70
57 is	60	68 is	70	49 is	50	35 is	40
82 is	80	37 is	40	22 is	20	52 is	50
46 is	50	26 is	30	85 is	90	99 is	100
43 is	40	51 is	50	78 is	80	29 is	30

Write these numbers to the nearest 100.

386 is	400	224 is	200	825 is	800	460 is	500
539 is	500	429 is	400	378 is	400	937 is	900
772 is	800	255 is	300	549 is	500	612 is	600
116 is	100	750 is	800	618 is	600	990 is	1 000
940 is	900	843 is	800	172 is	200	868 is	900

Write these numbers to the nearest 1 000.

3 240 is	3 000	2 500 is	3 000	9 940 is	10 000	1 051 is	1 000
8 945 is	9 000	5 050 is	5 000	5 530 is	6 000	4 850 is	5 000
6 200 is	6 000	7 250 is	7 000	8 499 is	8 000	8 450 is	8 000
12 501 is	13 000	8 762 is	9 000	6 500 is	7 000	3 292 is	3 000
1 499 is	1 000	14 836 is	15 000	10 650 is	11 000	11 241 is	11 000

Rounding a number means identifying which number (usually powers of 10) it is closest to. Use of a number line may be helpful. Remind children that the convention for the halfway point, 0.5, 5, 50, 500, etc. is to round up.

★ Rounding decimals

Write these decimals to the nearest tenth.

6.23 is	6.2	6.27 is	6.3

If the second decimal place is a 5, we round up the first decimal place to the number above.

6.25 is	6.3

Write these decimals to the nearest tenth.

9.21 is	9.2	4.38 is	4.4	2.47 is	2.5
3.48 is	3.5	8.17 is	8.2	6.28 is	6.3
7.14 is	7.1	3.91 is	3.9	2.56 is	2.6
8.41 is	8.4	2.36 is	2.4	1.53 is	1.5

Write these decimals to the nearest tenth.

9.35 is	9.4	8.71 is	8.7	6.05 is	6.1
1.19 is	1.2	3.65 is	3.7	4.21 is	4.2
8.55 is	8.6	7.35 is	7.4	9.14 is	9.1
6.83 is	6.8	2.15 is	2.2	6.34 is	6.3

Write these decimals to the nearest tenth.

25.61 is	25.6	14.35 is	14.4	11.24 is	11.2
16.85 is	16.9	24.34 is	24.3	71.36 is	71.4
26.85 is	26.9	11.54 is	11.5	37.25 is	37.3
92.42 is	92.4	95.65 is	95.7	27.36 is	27.4
45.17 is	45.2	36.75 is	36.8	22.05 is	22.1

If the child experiences difficulty, point out that the significant digit to look at is in the second decimal place. The use of a number line may be helpful when the child is still unsure. In the second section, the convention is to round 0.5 up.